Stabat Mater

for

TWO SOPRANOS, ALTO, TENOR, AND BASS SOLI
AND FULL CHORUS OF MIXED VOICES
WITH PIANO ACCOMPANIMENT

by

Gioacchino Rossini

*Orchestral score and parts may be obtained
from the Publisher on rental.*

G. SCHIRMER, Inc.   NEW YORK

STABAT MATER.

No. 1.—INTRODUCTION.

CHORUS AND QUARTET.

Stabat mater dolorosa
Juxta crucem lacrymosa,
   Dum pendebat Filius.

No. 2.—AIR.—(Tenor.)

Cujus animam gementem
Contristantem et dolentem
   Pertransivit gladius.
O quam tristis et afflicta
Fuit illa benedicta
   Mater Unigeniti;
Quæ mœrebat, et dolebat
Et tremebat, cum videbat
   Nati pœnas inclyti.

No. 3.—DUET.—(1st & 2nd Soprano.)

Quis est homo qui non fleret
Christi matrem si videret
   In tanto supplicio?
Quis non posset contristari
Piam matrem contemplari
   Dolentem cum Filio?

No. 4.—AIR.—(Bass.)

Pro peccatis suæ gentis
Vidit Jesum in tormentis,
   Et flagellis subditum.
Vidit suum dulcem natum
Morientem desolatum
   Dum emisit spiritum.

No. 5.—RECITATIVE (Bass) AND CHORUS.

(Without Accompaniment.)

Eia, mater, fons amoris,
Me sentire vim doloris
   Fac, ut tecum lugeam.
Fac ut ardeat cor meum
In amando Christum Deum,
   Ut sibi complaceam.

No. 6.—QUARTET.

Sancta mater, istud agas,
Crucifixi fige plagas
   Corde meo valide.
Tui nati vulnerati,
Tam dignati pro me pati,
   Pœnas mecum divide.
Fac me vere tecum flere
Crucifixo condolere,
   Donec ego vixero.
Juxta crucem tecum stare,
Te libenter sociare
   In planctu desidero.
Virgo, virginum præclara,
Mihi jam non sis amara,
   Fac me tecum plangere.

No. 7.—CAVATINA.—(2nd Soprano.)

Fac ut portem Christi mortem,
Passionis ejus sortem,
   Et plagas recolere
Fac me plagis vulnerari,
Cruce hâc inebriari,
   Ob amorem Filii.

No. 8.—AIR (1st Soprano) AND CHORUS.

Inflammatus et accensus
Per te, Virgo, sim defensus
   In die judicii.
Fac me cruce custodiri,
Morte Christi præmuniri,
   Confoveri gratiâ.

No. 9.—QUARTET.

(Without Accompaniment.)

Quando corpus morietur,
Fac ut animæ donetur
   Paradisi gloria.

No. 10.—FINALE.

In sempiterna sæcula.   Amen.

TRIBULATION
Words adapted by W. Ball

No. 1.—INTRODUCTION.
CHORUS AND QUARTET.

Lord most holy! Lord most mighty!
Righteous ever are Thy judgments.
Hear and save us, for Thy mercies' sake.

No 2.—AIR.—(TENOR.)

Lord! vouchsafe Thy loving-kindness,
Hear me in my supplication,
 And consider my distress.
Lo! my spirit fails within me,
Oh! regard me with compassion,
 And forgive me all my sin!
Let Thy promise be my refuge,
Oh, be gracious and redeem me,
 Save me from eternal death!

No. 3.—DUET.—(1st AND 2nd SOPRANO.)

Power eternal! Judge and Father!
 Who shall blameless stand before Thee,
 Or who Thy dreadful anger fly!
Hear, and aid us strength to gather
 To obey Thee, still adore Thee,
 In hope and faith to die!

No. 4.—AIR.—(BASS.)

Through the darkness Thou wilt lead me,
In my trouble Thou wilt heed me,
 And from danger set me free.
Lord! Thy mercy shall restore me,
And the day-spring shed before me,
 All salvation comes from Thee!

No. 5.—RECITATIVE (BASS) AND CHORUS.
(Without Accompaniment.)

Thou hast tried our hearts towards Thee; but if Thou wilt not forsake us, our souls shall fear no ill.

Lord! we pray Thee, help Thy people; save, O save them; make them joyful, and bless Thine inheritance.

No. 6.—QUARTET.

I have longed for Thy salvation, and my hope was in Thy goodness! Blessed be Thy Name, O Lord, for ever!

Now and henceforth, we beseech Thee, turn our hearts to Thy commandments, and incline them evermore to keep Thy law.

Give Thy servants understanding, so that they may shun temptation, and in all things follow Thee.

Oh! vouchsafe us true repentance, teach us always to obey Thee, and to walk the way of peace.

 Let Thy light so shine before us,
 And Thy mercy be upon us,
  Ev'n as is our trust in Thee.

No. 7.—CAVATINA.—(2nd SOPRANO.)

I will sing of Thy great mercy, for I was in deep affliction, and Thou didst deliver me. I will call unto the people, and the nations all shall hear me, and shall praise Thy holy Name!

No. 8—AIR (1st SOPRANO) AND CHORUS.

When Thou comest to the judgment, Lord, remember Thou Thy servants! None else can deliver us.

Save, and bring us to Thy kingdom, there to worship with the faithful, and for ever dwell with Thee!

No. 9.—QUARTET.
(Without accompaniment.)

Hear us, Lord! We bless the Name of our Redeemer! and His great and wondrous mercies now and ever glorify!

No. 10.—FINALE.

To Him be glory evermore. Amen.

№ 1. Introduction.

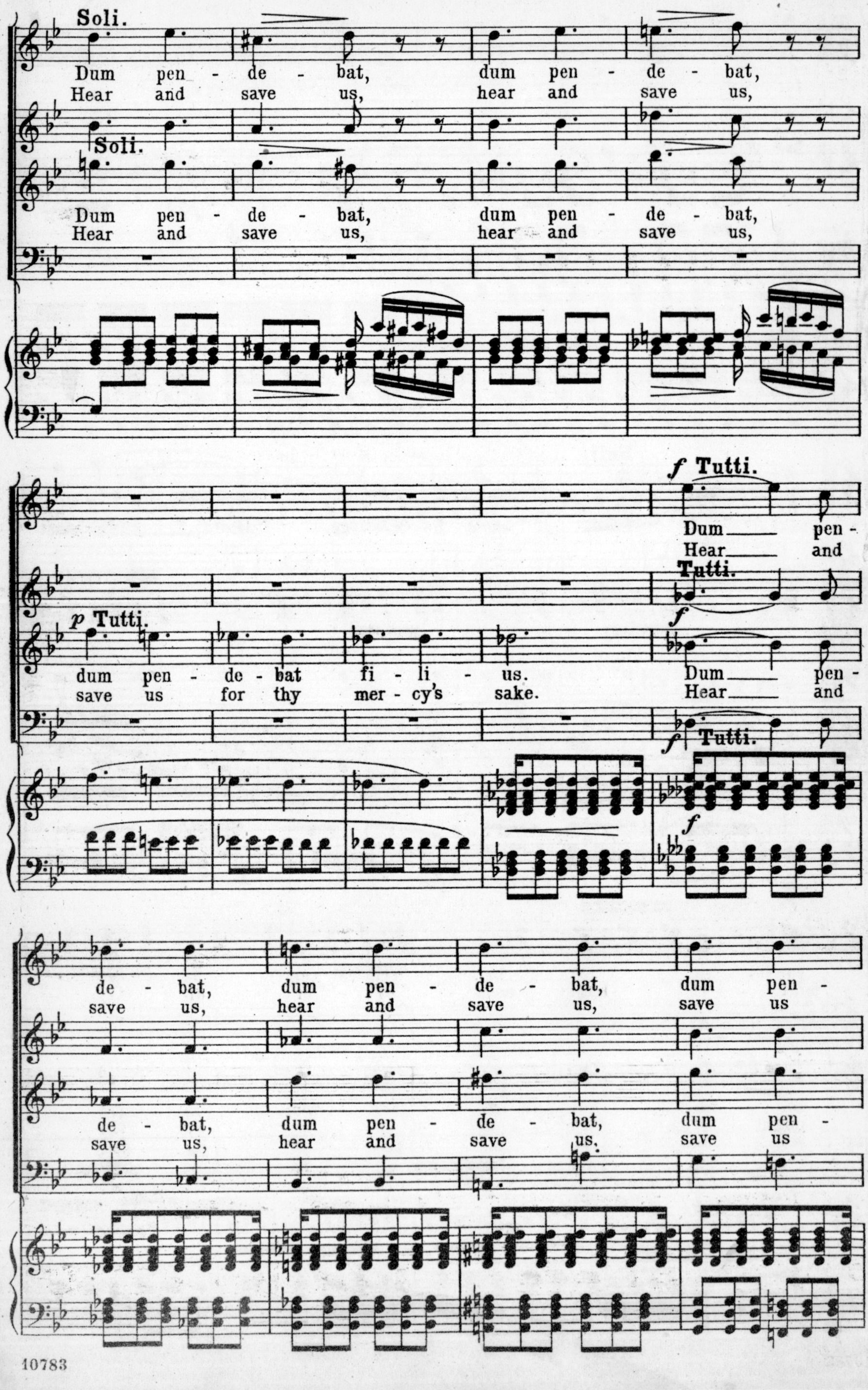
Soli.
Dum pen - de - bat, dum pen - de - bat,
Hear and save us, hear and save us,
Soli.
Dum pen - de - bat, dum pen - de - bat,
Hear and save us, hear and save us,
f Tutti.
Dum pen-
Hear and
Tutti.
p Tutti.
dum pen - de - bat fi - li - us. Dum pen-
save us for thy mer-cy's sake. Hear and
Tutti.
de - bat, dum pen - de - bat, dum pen-
save us, hear and save us, save us
de - bat, dum pen - de - bat, dum pen-
save us, hear and save us, save us

de - - bat   fi - - li -
for   thy   mer - - cy's

de - - bat   fi - - li -
for   thy   mer - - cy's

us.   Sta - bat ma - ter   do - - lo -
sake. Lord, most ho - ly,   Lord, most

Sta - bat ma - ter   do - - lo -
sake. Lord, most ho - ly,   Lord, most

ro - sa jux - ta cru - cem la - cry -
might - y! Right - eous ev - er are thy

ro - sa jux - ta cru - cem la - cry -
might - y! Right - eous ev - er are thy

Nº 4. "Pro Peccatis."
(Through the darkness.)
Air.

Allegretto maestoso. (♩= 88.)

Pro—— pec - ca - tis su - ae—— gen - tis vi - dit
Through the— darkness thou—— wilt lead me, In—— my

Je - sum in—— tor - men - tis, et—— fla - gel - lis
troub-le thou—— wilt heed me, And—— from dan-ger

sotto voce.

tum.
free.

Vi - dit
Lord! thy

sotto voce.

su - um dul - cem na - tum mo - ri - entem
mer - cy shall re - store me, And the day-spring

de - so - la - tum dum e - mi - sit
shed be - fore me, All sal - va - tion

tr
spi - ri - tum.
comes from thee.
pp
ff
ff
Vi - dit su - um dul - cem - na - tum mo - ri -
Lord! thy mer - cy shall re - store me, And the
3
3
3
pp
3
3
en - tem de - so - la - tum dum e - mi - sit,
day - spring shed be - fore me, All sal - va - tion,
dum e - mi - sit, dum e - mi - sit spi - ri -
all sal - va - tion, all sal - va - tion comes from
f
p
tum. vi - dit su - um dul - cem
thee. Lord! thy mer - cy shall re -
3
3
3

na - tum, mo - ri - en - tum de - so -
store me, and the day - spring shed be -

la - tum dum e - mi - sit, dum e -
fore me, all sal - va - tion, all sal -

mi - sit spi - ri - tum, vi - dit
va - tion comes from thee! Lord! thy

su - um dul - cem na - tum mo - ri -
mer - cy shall re - store me, and the

en - tem de - so - la - tum dum e - mi - sit,
day - spring shed be - fore me, all sal - va - tion,

dum e- — -mi- -sit spi- — -ri-
all sal- — -va- -tion comes from

tum, e- — -mi- sit, e- — -mi- sit
thee, all, all sal- -va- -tion

spi- — -ri- -tum, e- — -mi- sit,
comes from thee, all, all sal-

e- — -mi- sit spi- — -ri- -tum.
va- -tion comes from thee.

Nº 5. "Eia mater."
(Thou hast tried our hearts.)
Chorus and Recitative.

Andante mosso.

Bass (f): E - ia, ma-ter fons a - mo - ris, me sen-ti - re vim do-
Thou hast tried our hearts tow-ard, thee; But if thou wilt not for

Andante mosso. (♩= 76.)
Piano. (ad lib.)

lo - ris fac, ut__ te__ cum__ lu__-ge-
sake us, Our souls__ shall__ fear,__ shall fear__ no

10783

sotto voce.
Fac ut ar - de - at cor me - - -um,
Lord! we pray thee, spare thy peo - - -ple,
sotto voce.
Fac ut ar - de - at cor
Lord! we pray thee, help thy
sotto voce.
Fac ut ar - de - at cor
Lord! we pray thee, help thy
sotto voce.
am.
ill.
mf
In a - man - do Chris-tum De - - -um,
Save, O save them; make them joy - - -ful,
me - um,
peo - ple;
In a - man - do Chris-tum
Save, O save them; make them
me - um,
peo - ple;
In a - man - do Chris-tum
Save, O save them; make them

Andante mosso.
Christum De-um, ut si-bi com-
make them joy-ful, and bless thine in-
Christum De-um, ut si-bi com-pla-ce-
make them joy-ful, and bless thine in-her-i-
Christum De-um, ut si-bi com-pla-ce-
make them joy-ful, and bless thine in-her-i-
Andante mosso. (♩= 76.)
pla-ce-am, ut si-bi com-pla-ce-am,
her-i-tance, and bless thine in-her-i-tance,
am, ut si-bi com-pla-ce-am,
tance, and bless thine in-her-i-tance,
am, ut si-bi com-pla-ce-am,
tance, and bless thine in-her-i-tance,

39

Allegro moderato.
am, in a- -man-do Chris-tum,
tance, save them, save them, make them,
am, in a- -man-do Chris-tum,
tance, save them, save them, make them,
am, in a- -man-do Chris-tum,
tance, save them, save them, make them,
Allegro moderato. (♪ = 126.)
mf
Andante mosso.
De-um, ut si-bi com-pla-ce-am,
joy-ful, and bless thine in-her-i-tance,
De-um, ut si-bi com-pla- -ce- am,
joy-ful, and bless thine in-her- -i- -tance,
De-um, ut si-bi com-pla- -ce- am,
joy-ful, and bless thine in-her- -i- -tance,
Andante mosso. (♩ = 76.)

41

Adagio.
sotto voce.
ut si - bi com - pla - - - - ce-
and bless thine in - her - - - - i-
sotto voce.
ut si - bi com - pla - ce-
and bless thine in - her - i-
sotto voce
sotto voce.
ut si - bi com - pla - ce-
and bless thine in - her - i-
sotto voce.
Adagio.
p sotto voce.
am, ut si - bi com - pla - ce - am.
tance, and bless thine in - her - i - tance.
am, ut si - bi com - pla - ce - am.
tance, and bless thine in - her - i - tance.
am, ut si - bi com - pla - ce - am.
tance, and bless thine in - her - i - tance.

No. 6. "Sancta mater, Istud agas.
(I have longed for thy Salvation.)
Quartet.

44

a - gas, cru-ci-fix-i fi-ge pla - - gas,
va - - tion, and my hope was in thy good- -ness,

Cor-de me-o, cor-de me- - -o va-li-
Bless-ed be Thy name, O Lord, for ev-

de, cor-de me-o, cor-de me-o,
er! Bless-ed be Thy name, Thy ho-ly

cor-de me-o va- -li-de.
name, O Lord, for ev- -er.

10783

45

46

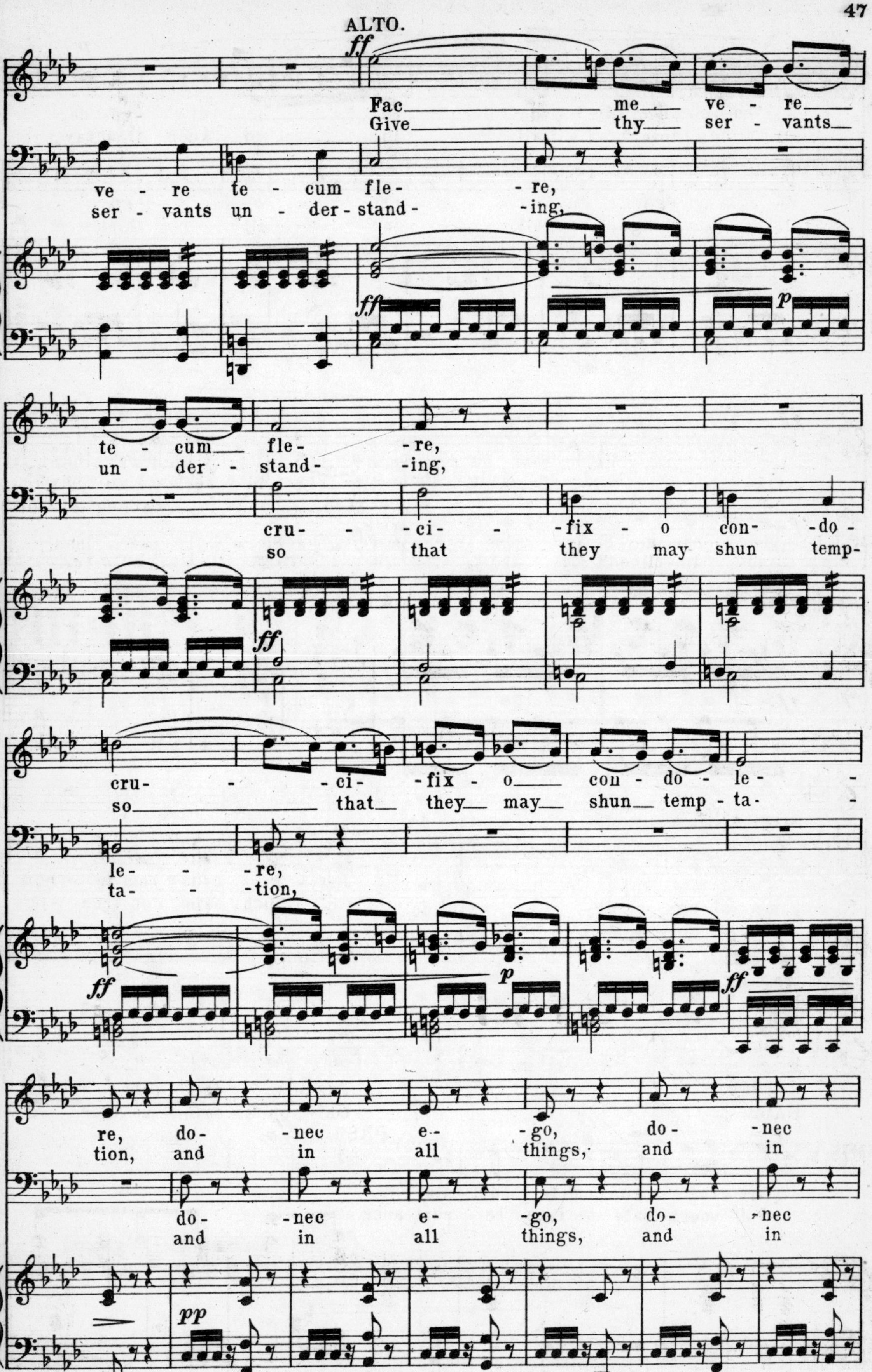
ALTO.
Fac me ve - re
Give thy ser - vants
ve - re te - cum fle - re,
ser - vants un - der - stand - ing,
te - cum fle - re,
un - der - stand - ing,
cru - ci - fix - o con - do -
so that they may shun temp -
cru - ci - fix - o con - do - le -
so that they may shun temp - ta -
le - re,
ta - tion,
re, do - nec e - go, do - nec
tion, and in all things, and in
do - nec e - go, do - nec
and in all things, and in

e- -go, do- -nec e- -go
all things, all in all things
e- -go, do- -nec e- -go
all things, all in all things
ff
vix- - - - -e-ro, do-nec-e-go vix-e-
fol- - - - -low thee, and in allthings fol-low
ff
vix- - - - -e-ro.
fol- - - - -low thee.
ff
p
SOPRANO.
p
Jux-ta cru-cem te-cum
Oh! vouch-safe us true re-
ALTO.
ro.
thee.
TENOR.
p
Jux-ta cru-cem te-cum
Oh! vouch-safe us true re-
BASS.
p
Jux-ta cru-cem te-cum sta-re,
Oh! vouch-safe us true re-pent-ance,
pp

sta - re, te li - ben - ter so - ci -
pen - tance, teach us al - ways to o -
Te li - ben - ter so - ci - a - re,
Teach us al - ways to o - bey thee,
sta - re, te li - ben - ter so - ci -
pen - tance, teach us al - ways to o -
a - re.
bey thee.
te li - ben - ter so - ci -
teach us al - ways to o -
a - re.
bey thee.
Jux - ta cru - cem te - cum sta - re,
Oh! vouch - safe us true re - pen - tance,
a - re,
bey thee,
in planc - tu de - si - de - ro,
and to walk the way of peace,

ALTO.
In planc - tu de-
and to walk the
TENOR.
In planctu, in
of peace, the way
de - si - de - ro. In planctu, in
the way of peace, of peace, the way
p
- si - de - ro, in planc - tu de - si - de
way of peace, and to walk the way of
f
plane - tu, in planc - tu de - si - de
of peace, and to walk the way of
SOPRANO. p
in planctu, in planctu,
to walk the way,
ro, in planctu, in planctu,
peace, to walk the way,
ro, in planctu, in planctu,
peace, to walk the way,
cresc.

in planc - tu de - si - de - ro.
and walk the way, the way of peace.

in planc - tu de - si - de - ro.
and walk the way, the way of peace.

Virgo, virginum praeclara, mihi jam non sis a-
Let thy light so shine before us, And thy mercy be up-

Virgo, virginum praeclara, mihi jam non sis a-
Let thy light so shine before us, And thy mercy be up-

52

ma - ra; Vir - go, vir-gi-num prae-cla - ra,
on us; let thy light so shine be - fore us,

mi - hi jam non sis a - ma - ra, fac me te -
and thy mer-cy be up - on us, e'en as is

cum plan - ge - re, fac me
our trust in thee, e'en as

10783

te - cum plan - ge - re:
is our trust in thee:
te - cum plan - ge - re:
is our trust in thee:
Vir - go, vir - gi - num prae - cla - ra,
Let thy light so shine be - fore us,
Vir - go, vir - gi - num prae-
Let thy light so shine be-
Vir - go, vir - gi - num prae - cla - ra,
Let thy light so shine be - fore us,
Vir - go, vir - gi - num prae-
Let thy light so shine be-
p
mi - hi jam non sis a - ma - ra,
and thy mer - cy be up - on us,
cla - ra,
fore us,
mi - hi jam non sis a-
and thy mer - cy be up-
mi - hi jam non sis a - ma - ra,
and thy mer - cy be up - on us,
cla - ra,
fore us,
mi - hi jam non sis a-
and thy mer - cy be up-

54

— te - cum, — fac me — te - cum, fac me te - cum plan - ge-
— is our — trust in — thee, — e'en as is our trust in
fac me te - cum, fac me te - cum plan - ge-
our trust in thee, e'en as is our trust in
— te - cum, fac me — te - cum, fac me te - cum plan - ge-
— is our trust in — thee, — e'en as is our trust in
fac me te - cum, fac me te - cum plan - ge-
our trust in thee, e'en as is our trust in
re, fac me te - cum plan-ge - re,
thee, as is our trust in thee,
re, fac me te-cum
thee, e'en as is our
re, fac me te - cum plan-ge - re,
thee, e'en as is our trust in thee,
re, fac me te-cum
thee, e'en as is our
plan - - ge - re,
as — our trust
plan-ge - re
trust in thee,
plan - - ge - re,
as — our trust
plan-ge - re
trust in thee,

56

Nº 7. "Fac ut portem."
(I will sing of thy great mercy.)
Cavatina.

Andante grazioso. (♩= 104.)

Fac ut por-tem Chris-ti mor-tem, pas-si-o - nis e - jus
I will sing of thy great mer-cy, for I was in deep af-

sor-tem et pla-gas re-co-le — re,
flic-tion, and thou didst de-liv-er me,

et _____ pla-gas
Lord, _____ thou didst

re — — — — — co'-le — re.
de — — — — — liv-er me!

Fac me pla - gis vul - ne - ra - ri,
I will call un - to the peo - ple,

cru - ce hâc i - ne - bri - a - ri,
and the na - tions all shall hear me,

ob a - mo - rem Fi - li -
and shall praise thy ho - ly

i, ob a - mo - rem Fi - li -
name, and shall praise thy ho - ly

i, ob a - mo - ram Fi - li - i: fac me
name, and shall praise thy ho - ly name: I will

pla - gis vul - ne - ra - ri, cru - ce hâc i - ne - bri -
call un - to the peo - ple, and the na - tions all shall

a - ri, ob a - mo - rem Fi - li - i,
hear me, and shall praise thy ho - ly name,

ob a - mo -
all shall praise
rem Fi - li -
thy ho - ly
i, ob a - mo - - rem
name, all shall praise thy
Fi - li i.
ho - ly name.
f
p
f
ff
p
p

Nº 8. "Inflammatus et accensus."
(When thou comest.)
Air and Chorus.

ma - tus et ac - cen - sus
com - est to the judg - ment,

per - te, Vir - go, sim de -
Lord, re - mem - ber thou thy

fen - sus, per - te, Vir - go,
ser - vants, O re - mem - ber

sim de - fen - sus in di - e ju -
thou thy ser - vants, none else can de -

di - - - - - - ci - i.
liv - - - - - - er us.

10783

cru - ce cus - to - di - ri,
bring us to thy king - dom,

sotto voce.
Fac me cru - ce cus - to -
Save and bring us to thy

sotto voce.
Fac me cru - ce cus - to -
Save and bring us to thy

mor - te Christi prae - mu - ni - ri,
there to wor - ship with the faith - ful,

di - ri, mor - te
king - dom, there to

di - ri, mor - te
king - dom, there to

mor - te Chris - ti
there to wor - ship
Chris - ti prae - mu - ni - ri, mor - te
wor - ship with the faith - ful, there to
Chris - ti prae - mu - ni - ri, mor - te
wor - ship with the faith - ful, there to
prae - mu - ni - ri, con - fo -
with the faith - ful, and for
Chris - ti prae - mu - ni - ri,
wor - ship with the faith - ful,
Chris - ti prae - mu - ni - ri,
wor - ship with the faith - ful,

67

ti - â.
with thee.
gra - ti - â.
dwell with thee.
gra - ti - â.
dwell with thee.
f
In - flam - ma - tus,
When thou com - est,
sotto voce.
in - flam - ma - tus et ac -
when thou com - est to the
cen - sus, per te, Vir - go,
judg - ment, Lord, re - mem - ber

69

in di - e ju - di - ci - i, in di - e ju - di - ci - i, in di - e ju - di - ci - i.
none else can de - liv - er us, none else can de - liv - er us, none else can de - liv - er us.

Solo.
p sotto voce.

Fac me cruce custodiri,
Save, and bring us to thy kingdom,

sotto voce.
Fac me cruce custodiri,
Save, and bring us to thy kingdom,

sotto voce.
Fac me cruce custodiri,
Save, and bring us to thy kingdom,

sotto voce.

morte Christe praemuniri,
there to worship with the

ni - ri, mor - te
faith - ful, there to
mor - te Chris - ti prae - mu - ni - ri,
there to wor - ship with the faith - ful,
mor - te Chris - ti prae - mu - ni - ri,
there to wor - ship with the faith - ful,
Chris - ti prae - mu-ni - ri
wor - ship with the faith - ful,
mor - te Chris - ti prae - mu-
there to wor - ship with the
mor - te Chris - ti prae - mu-
there to wor - ship with the

73

- - - - ti - â,
with thee,
ve - ri gra - ti - â,
ev - er dwell with thee,
ve - ri gra - ti - â, con - fo -
ev - er dwell with thee, and for
ff
p
con - fo -
and for
con - fo - ve - ri
and for ev - er
ve - ri gra - - - - - -
ev - er dwell

ve - - - - ri gra - - - - ti -
ev - - - - er dwell with
gra - - - - - - ti - - -
dwell with
- - - - - - - - - ti - - -
with
â,
thee,
con - fo -
and for
â,
thee,
con - fo - ve - ri
and for ev - er
â,
thee,
con - fo - ve - ri
and for ev - er
gra - - - - -
dwell

76

N⁰ 9. "Quando corpus."
(Hear us, Lord.)
Quartet (without accompaniment.)

ne - tur, a - ni - mae — do - ne - tur Pa - ra - di - si
mer - cies, all his won - drous mer - cies, now and ev - er
ne - tur, a - ni - mae do - ne - tur
mer - cies, all his won - drous mer - cies,
ff
sotto voce.
glo - ri - a. Quan - do
glo - ri - fy. Bless the
ff
ff
sotto voce.
Pa - ra - di - si glo - ri - a. Quan - do
now and ev - er glo - ri - fy! Bless the
ff
ff
ff
p
cor - pus mo - ri - e - tur, fac ut a - ni - mae do -
name of our Re - deem - er, and his great and won - drous
cor - pus mo - ri - e - tur, fac ut a - ni - mae do -
name of our Re - deem - er, and his great and won - drous

pp
ne - tur Pa - ra - di - si, Pa - ra - di - si glo - ri -
mer - cies, now and ev - er, now and ev - er. glo - ri -
pp
ne - tur Pa - ra - di - si, Pa - ra - di - si glo - ri -
mer - cies, now and ev - er, now and ev - er glo - ri -
pp
pp
sotto voce.
a. Quan - do cor - pus mo - ri - e - tur,
fy! All his mer - cies, all his mer - cies,
sotto voce.
a. Quan - do cor - pus mo - ri - e - tur,
fy! All his mer - cies, all his mer - cies,
p
f
fac - ut a - ni - mae do - ne - tur Pa - ra - di - si
all his great and won - drous mer - cies, now and ev - er
f
fac - ut a - ni - mae do - ne - tur
all his great and won - drous mer - cies,
f
f

sotto voce.
glo - ri - a. Quan - do
glo - ri - fy! Bless the
sotto voce.
Pa - ra - di - si glo - ri - a. Quan - do
now and ev - er glo - ri - fy! Bless the
corpus mo - ri - e - tur, fac ut a - ni - mae do - ne - tur Pa - ra -
name of our Re - deem - er, and his great and won - drous mer - cies now and
corpus mo - ri - e - tur, fac ut a - ni - mae do - ne - tur Pa - ra -
name of our Re - deem - er, and his great and won - drous mer - cies now and
di - si, Pa - ra - di - si glo - ri - a. Quan - do
ev - er, now and ev - er glo - ri - fy, all his
di - si, Pa - ra - di - si glo - ri - a. Quan - do
ev - er, now and ev - er glo - ri - fy, all his

ff
cor-pus mo-ri-e-tur, fac ut a-ni-mae do-ne
mer-cies, all his mer-cies, all his great and wondrous mer
a-ni-mae do-ne
great and wondrous mer
cor-pus mo-ri-e-tur, fac ut a-ni-mae do-ne
mer-cies, all his mer-cies, all his great and wondrous mer
sotto voce
tur Pa-ra-di-si, Pa-ra-di-si glo-ri
cies now and ev-er, now and ev-er glo-ri
tur Pa-ra-di-si, Pa-ra-di-si glo-ri
cies now and ev-er, now and ev-er glo-ri
glo-ri
glo-ri
p
a. Quan-do cor-pus mo-ri-e-tur, fac ut a-ni-mae do
fy, all his mer-cies, all his mercies, all his great and wondrous
a-ni
great and
a. Quan-do cor-pus mo-ri-e-tur, fac ut a-ni
fy, all his mer-cies, all his mercies, all his great and

10783

ne - - - tur Paradisi, Paradisi glo -
mer - - cies now and ev - er, now and ev - er glo -

mae do - ne - tur Paradisi, Pa-ra-di-si glo -
wondrous mer - cies now and ev - er, now and ev - er glo -

mae do - ne - tur Pa-ra-di-si, Pa-ra-di-si glo -
wondrous mer - cies now and ev - er, now and ev - er glo -

- ri - a,
- ri - fy,

- ri - a, Pa - ra -
- ri - fy, now and

- ri - a, Pa - ra - di - si, Pa - ra -
- ri - fy, now and ev - er, now and

glo - ri - a, Pa - ra - di - si glo - ri - a, Pa - ra -
glo - ri - fy, now and ev - er glo - ri - fy, now and

83

Nº 10. "In sempiterna saecula, Amen."
(To Him be Glory evermore.)
Chorus.

(The four Solo parts with the Chorus.)

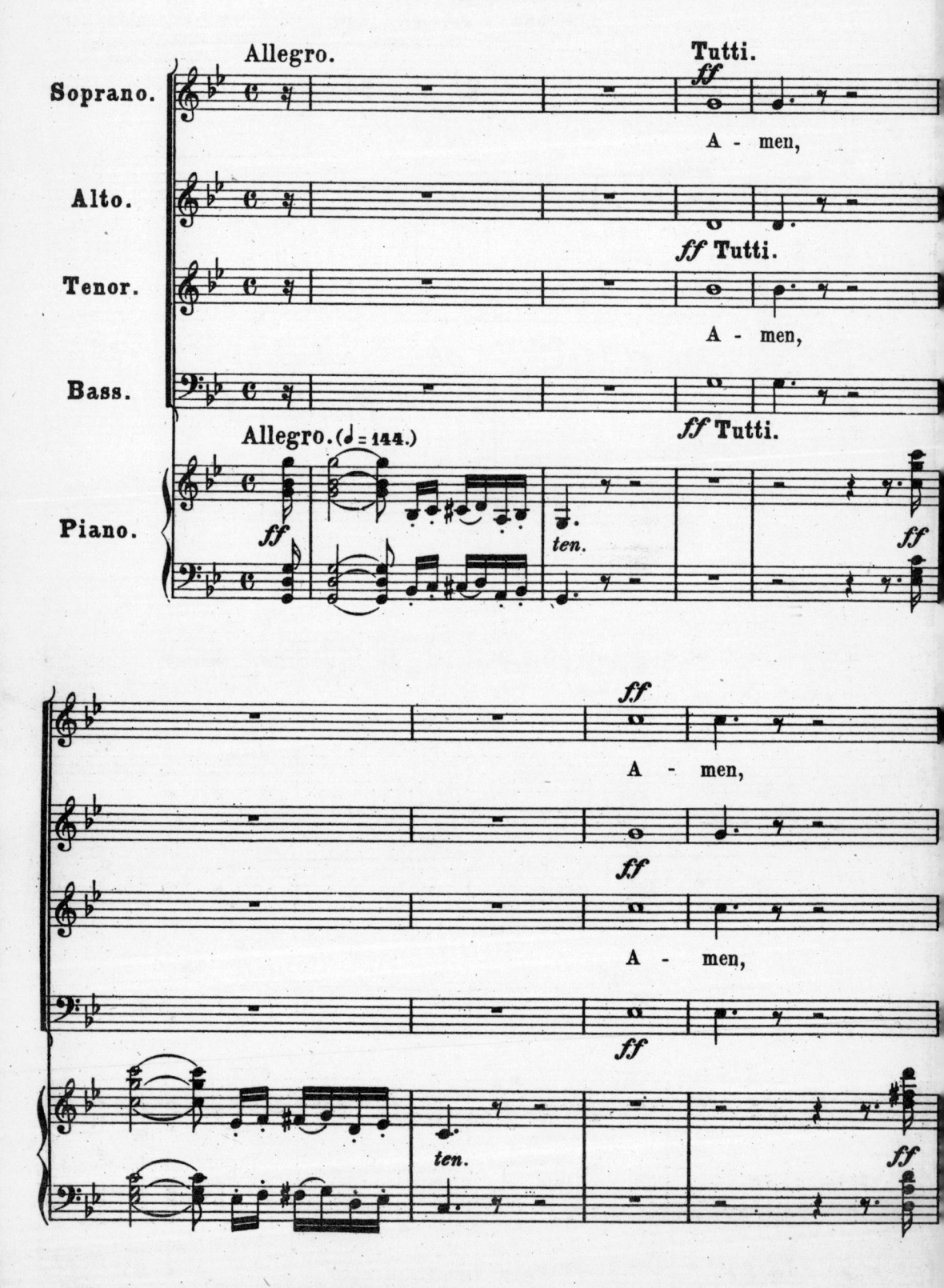

ff
f
A - men,
In sem-pi-ter - na
To him be glo-ry
A - men,
ten.
sae-cu - la, A - - - - men, A -
ev - er - more,
Iu sem-pi-ter - na
To him be glo - ry
A - - - - men, A -
men,
sae-cu - la, A - - - men, A -
ev - er - more,
men, in sempi-ter - na
to him be glo - ry
A - - - men, A -

A - - - - - - - - - - men, A - - -
- - - - - - - - - - - - men,
sae-cu-la, A - - - - - - - men, A - - -
ev-er-more,
- - - - - - - - - - - - men, in sem-pi-ter-na
to him be glo-ry
- - - - - - - - - - men, in sempi-ter - na
to him be glo - ry
A. - - - - - - - - men,
- - - - - - - - - - men, in sempi-
to him be
sae-cu-la, A - - - - - - -
ev-er-more,
sae - cu - la, A - men, A - men,
ev - er - more, A - men, A - men,
A - men, in sem-pi-ter - na sae - cu -
to him be glo - - ry ev - er -
ter-na sae - cu - la, in sem-pi-ter-na sae -
glo-ry ev - er - more, to him be glo-ry ev -
- men, A - - - - - men,

in sem-pi-ter - na sae - cu - la, A -
to him be glo - ry ev - er - more, A -
la, A - men, A-men, in sem-pi-ter - na
more, A - men, A-men, to him be glo - ry
cu - la, in sem-pi-ter-na sae - cu - la, in sem-pi-
er - more, to him be glo - ry ev - er-more, to him
A - men, A -
men, A-men, in sem-pi-ter - na sae - cu -
men, A-men, to him be glo - ry ev - er -
sae - cu - la, A - men, A-men,
ev - er - more, A - men, A-men,
ter-na sae - cu - la, in sem-pi - ter-na sae -
glo-ry ev - er - more, to him be glo-ry ev -
men, A - men,
la, in sem-pi-ter - na sae-cu-la, A -
more, to him be glo - ry ev-er-more A -
in sem-pi-ter - na, A -
to him be glo - ry, A -
cu - la, A - men, A -
er - more A - men, A -
A -

men, A
in sem-pi-ter - na sae-cu-la,
men, to him be glo - ry ev - er-more, A
men, A
men, A
in sem-pi-ter - na sae - cu
men, to him be glo - ry ev - er
men, A-men
men, in sempi - ter-na sae
to him be glo-ry ev
men,
ff
la, A - men, A - men, in sem-pi-ter - na
more, to him be glo - ry
in sem-pi-ter - na sae - cu - la,
to him be glo - ry ev - er - more, A
cu - la, in sem-pi - ter-na sae - cu - la, in sem-pi
er - more, to him be glo - ry ev - er - more, to him be
A - men, A

89

na, in sempi-ter - - na, in sempi-ter - - na, in sempi-ter - -
ry, to him be glo - - ry, to him be glo - - ry, to him be glo - -
men, A - men, A - - - - - - - men, A -
na, in sempi-ter - - na, in sempi-ter - - na, in sempi-ter - -
ry, to him be glo - - ry, to him be glo - - ry, to him be glo - -
men, A - men, A - - - - - - - men, A -
na, A - - - - - - -
ry,
men, A - - - - - - - -
na,
ry, A - - - - - -
pp

men, in sem-pi-ter - na
to him be glo - ry
men, in sem-pi-to him be
men,
sae - cu - la, A
ev - er - more,
ter - na sae - cu - la, A
glo - ry ev - er - more,
in sem-pi-ter - na sae - cu-
to him be glo - ry ev - er-
in sem-pi-ter - na sae - cu - la,
to him be glo - ry ev - er - more,
cresc.
f
ff
men, A
men, A
la,
more,
A
A
men,
ff

men, A - - - - - - - - - - - -
- - - - - - men, A - - - - -
- - - men, A - - - - - - - - - -
A - - - - - - - - - men, A
men, in sempi - ter - na, in sem - pi - ter - na,
to him be glo - ry, to him be glo - ry,
men, in sem - pi - ter - na, in sem - pi - ter - na,
to him be glo - ry, to him be glo - ry,
men, in sem - pi - ter - na, in sem - pi -
to him be glo - ry, to him be
p
in sempi - ter - na, in sempi - ter - na, in sempi - ter -
to him be glo - ry, to him be glo - ry, to him be glo -
in sempi - ter - na, in sempi - ter - na, in sempi -
to him be glo - ry, to him be glo - ry, to him be
ter - na, in sem - pi - ter - na, A - men,
glo - ry, to him be glo - ry,
cresc. - - -
f
ff

na, A
ry,
ter na, A
glo ry,
in sem-pi-ter na, A
to him be glo ry,
in sem-pi ter na, A
to him be glo ry,
men, in sem-pi-ter na sae
men, to him be glo ry ev
in sem-pi ter na sae
men, to him be glo ry ev
in sem-pi-ter na
men, to him be glo ry
in sem-pi
to him be
p
cresc.
cu-la, A
er-more,
cu-la, A
er-more,
sae cu la,
ev er more,
ter na sae cu la, A
glo ry ev er more,
f
ff
ff

men, A - - - men, A -
- men, A - - -
A - - - men,
- - - men, A -
- men, in sem-pi-ter - na,
to him be glo - ry,
- men, A - men, in sem-pi-ter - na,
to him be glo - ry,
A - men, in sem-pi-ter - na,
to him be glo - ry,
- men, A - men, in sem-pi-
to him be
in sem-pi-ter - na, in sem-pi-ter - na,
to him be glo - ry, to him be glo - ry,
in sem-pi-ter - na, in sem-pi-ter - na,
to him be glo - ry, to him be glo - ry,
ter - na, in sem - pi - ter - na, in sem-pi-
glo - ry, to him be glo - ry, to him be
p
cresc.

95

men, in sem - pi - ter - - - na, in sem - pi - ter - - -
to him be glo - - - ry, to him be glo - - -
men, A - - men, A - - men, A - - men, A - - -
men, in sem - pi - ter - - - na, in sem - pi - ter - - -
to him be glo - - - ry, to him be glo - - -
men, A - - men, A - - men, A - men, A - - -
ff
na, in sem - pi - ter - - - na, in sem - pi - ter - - -
ry, to him be glo - - - ry, to him be glo - - -
na, in sem - pi - ter - - - na, in sem - pi - ter - - -
ry, to him be glo - - - ry, to him be glo - - -
na.
ry.
men.
na.
ry.
men.

97

Tempo I. Animato.
ff
men, in sempi-ter - - - - na, in sempi-ter -
men, to him be glo - - - - ry, to him be glo -
men, A - - - - -
men, in sempi-ter - - - -
to him be glo - - - -
men, A - - - - -
Tempo I. Animato.
ff
na, ry,
na, in sempi-ter - - - - - na,
ry, to him be glo - - - - - ry
A - - - - - - - men, in sempi-ter -
men, to him be glo -
men, A -
A - - - - - - - men,
men, A -

na, in sempi-ter - - - - - - - - - - - -
ry, to him be glo - - - - - - - - - - -

in sempi - ter - - - - - - - - - - na, in sempi - ter - -
to him be glo - - - - - - - - - - ry, to him be glo - -

- - - - na, A -
- - - - ry,

- - - - na, A -
- - - - ry,

- - - men, A - men, A -

- - - men, A - men, A -

ff

men, A - - men, A -

men, A - - men, A -